Singing Riptide

Singing Riptide

Poems

Cheryl Wilder

Press 53
Winston-Salem

Press 53, LLC
PO Box 30314
Winston-Salem, NC 27130

First Edition

Cover art, *Singing Riptide*, Copyright © 2025 by Coleen Tagnolli
Used by permision of the artist

Author photo Copyright © 2025 by Charles Gupton

Library of Congress Control Number
2025939377

ISBN 978-1-950413-99-7

For Taliesin, Evander, and Roland.
And the many worlds you've made possible.

A better world has gotta start somewhere.
Why not with you and me?

—Tom Robbins

Contents

Prologue

Anything That Happens, the companion to this volume, tells the story of the event that rooted me in shame and how I navigated the immediate aftermath.

In 1994, when I was twenty, a friend and I went out for an evening of dancing. It was my first time drinking in a bar. At the end of the night, as we walked down the street, we tossed the car keys back and forth. I'm the one who slid into the driver's seat.

We didn't make it home.

I lost control of the car, and it slammed into a pole. My friend was taken to the hospital and woke from a coma four months later with a life-altering brain injury. I was taken to jail.

Section I

Every instant the world we know splits
into an infinite number of other worlds,
different futures and different pasts.

—Richard Bach

Learning to Forgive

1)

Feed iron-bearing river sand
into a tatara stoked to 2500°.
Stir. Churn.
Don't waver. The first step
lasts as long as it lasts.

From fire,
the jewel of earth emerges—
tamahagane—pure steel in two parts:
Soft bearing power absorbs shock.
Hard resilience for a sharpened edge.

2)

Heat, hammer, fold—
a tedious task repeated; heat,
hammer, fold—strengthen;
heat, hammer, fold
—think balance. Think,
work the impurities out.
Release the slag.

3)

Shape yielding core
snug inside durable shell.

Heat.   Reinforce.   Quench.

A figure emerges:
curved spine; endurant
strength; wear-resistant edges.

4)

Fully formed,
a series of water
stones hone edges,
fine particles
remove steel,
finer and finer
remove less
and less.

It's critical not to falter.
One in three crack.

The Chapter of Accidents

Rewind the moment of impact:
Start the ignition.

Drink the first drink.
Answer the phone.

Replace esteem for desire.
Move away.

Father's absence. Mother's
coveted empty nest. Submerge

in water that swallows.
Risk the river's swiftness,

the cliff's edge.

right /rīt/

verb. Restore to a normal correct condition or situation: As in, there is no way to *right* the crash. Nothing to turn back over. We didn't capsize as much as we shattered. I want to *right* my life, meaning, I want to hug my friend until we fall over, jump in his car on the way to lunch shifts overlooking the ocean, be inside the weightlessness of a twenty-year-old body. But there is only a new normal, a new *correct condition*: My worth an open wound on the body of the masses.

For Years I Pull My Existence Out of Emptiness

Emptiness that fills a room,
lungs ballooned; throat rasped
by ridged edges, full abrasion of the senses.

Emptiness engorged with darkness
by which I mean
guilt, by which I mean

shame—
the way it holds on. Emptiness
from which I pull existence

with every slid-open eyelid
every morsel that quenches my lips

and every finger that touches quivering tenderness
at the valley of my hip. Emptiness.

I pull
with every thought of my last breath.

Law of Attraction

We fit. My shame needs
a man to reassure my worth

is nothing. His insecurity needs
a woman to fill his confidence

where boys are encouraged to conquer.
We marry. He breathes my worthlessness

alive—she saunters off his lips,
takes the coziest blanket; curls

on the couch. I see how vulnerable she is
in the hands of another,

scoop her from the cushion,
cradle her body as I

remove a piece of *lessness*,
begin our transformation.

For the Sake of Him, I Will

My crotch burns.
Under weight of a clean
sheet and thermal blankets
I shift my legs in unison

from one side of the bed
to the other, lift the wrist
with three paper bands, finger

the one that identifies me
as a baby boy's mother.

My uterus presses
to keep moving. Says aloud
with its insistent tug, *Go to him.*

In the nursery's wellspring of stillness,
the scent of awe rises.
My hands hold one another.
For the sake of him, I will

pardon my shame.
There is no other choice.
Chains and shackles are not allowed here.

Soft grunts escape
the landscape of his face,
birthed in velvet skin,
dark hair that matches eyes dancing
left and right and—

Hiiiiii, my cells coo,
calling to find their own.

Oceanfront

It's not a frantic scene, a woman unfolding
a pull-out couch, dragging it to wedge

between open balcony doors, unmaking
choices. Here, I begin a long goodbye

to the dissolution of a footnote
marriage—the final stop for despair's

harsh words. His. Mine. Below,
turtle hatchlings emerge, escape

predators under the night sky.
I crack open

refuge in this hotel respite,
awaken unshielded,

unbound, throw myself
into the mercy of uncertainty.

Critique

Eyeballs fall
between

strands of wet
hair as I shake

bent over
in the bathroom.

They roll on linoleum,
look at scars

on my big toe,
the one above my left knee.

Eyeballs fill
the bedside chair,

cover floorboards,
swallow words,

follow me
out the room,

down the street
until it's only

eyes everywhere,
watching.

I Am What I Can

We cannot doubt of our existence while we doubt.
—René Descartes

Some nights, all tasks inflate
to the top of my list. I grasp

to withstand the enveloped
sense of drowning: Transform

into a tickle monster, feed cats, nourish
bones and brain, my son's respect for women.

Start laundry, organize bills,
leave dishes until after

he brushes his teeth, and I read
stories and he asks me

back into his room three times
for food and food and water

which I bring before closing his door.
Clean the kitchen, leave clothes to wrinkle

and mildew, the cats pining
for their routine rubdown.

Check locks I know are latched,
tug at every closed window—

the last sentinel for the boy
who kicks off his sheets in his sleep.

In the hallway, nightlight clicks on.
Cats knead biscuits. I lie down,

bedroom door open, welcome
his climb into bed before dawn.

To Be of Use

Nietzsche says, *Be the poet of your life*,
resource and product, support

beams and breaks that hold
lines together. I assess

my value, cost
the price of not wanting more

than crafting economy rooms
however spacious the inside.

A spirit level promises balance.
Impact drills exercise structure.

Sometimes work draws blood
to find a pulse.

The Vertical Forward

Nothing keeps me from mirrors.
They surround us on the dance floor,

arms and legs swirling hours
before the crash exiled

my self-worth. Unmoored,
the South claims me,

the way the ocean births the sun
again, and again. I dig through *whys*,

search for ghost crabs, find Mom's voice
saying Dad moved out. I was seven,

in California, dancing to *Madonna*
alone in my room with mirrored closet-doors,

the spring of my toes touching
abandonment that is possibility.

Wilder Family Crest

A demi-lion. A wild man.
Gold and red garland means
achievement. Stateliness.

A shield to build upon promise,
a history that bore a father
who treated heirs like a prison

sentence or the daughters
we are, not killed at birth to save
the family shame, or adopted

overseas to save the family shame.
Nothing as brutal. The phone rang less.
One letter in the mail. Not showing up.

Graduation. Christmas. A new wife.
His career arresting bad guys,
the crest on his chest to serve and protect.

The power of paper and pen and time—
a shield against the shame my father
left me. I shout the Wilder motto,

Let the walls of power yield,
evoke courage and illumination.
Tie my limbs to the family tree.

Complaint of Shelter

after Richard Blanco

I was meant for all things to meet:
To carve place for protection;
dank cave, thatched roof of palm,
hands shaping mud and straw.
Welcome everyone out of the cold.

I kept watch over you, learned
constellations and your behaviors
by season. How you opened
doors to air out, or huddled against
winter sleet filling lungs.

First, you built walls
between you and the snow,
between you and wolves who'd eat you.
Then walls thicker, taller, until someone
built the strongest of their time,
creating others on both sides.

And then you were safe
from the outside built inwards,
segmented room into rooms, people
into person, daughter down the hall
door slammed and sealed shut,
no one to hear a cry for help,
including yours.

I've watched you turn
me into wilderness—power
feeding on the innocent
who run back outside
into the mouths of wolves,
hoping to escape the pain.

How small your landscape now,
dwellers reveling in privacy. I gave you
more than you bargained for:
Safety to quench your first cry.
A way to see yourself as separate.

Wilder Inheritance

Passed to me in three-ring binders,
my family tree built by the succession of sons.
In what orchard will I find the daughters?

There is no land, no single tree to sit under,
nowhere to rest. Maybe they're like me,
authoring their own stories, breaking bread

at kitchen tables. Where shall I begin?
My father erased himself unknowing
absence is an unwritten story

waiting to be told. I knew how to write
a check, board a Greyhound, learn family
history without my father

and yet, I'd settle to know his wrinkles.
The thickness of his medical chart.
Genetics, his last endowment to give.

(Dropping) The Female Line

In the land of my mother
a bull moans on a slow methodical

sunset walk through town.
With salt on my face, I drink

from the softness of my tongue.
I can't ignore those who want

the world to stop before all
bones are excavated.

Severed from a patrilineal line
like women before me

there is no twang of belonging
to a string of vocal patterns.

How do I know what to do
if no one shows me, Mother?

I throw salt over my left shoulder,
listen to the pulse

of matriarchal blood,
steady silence that fills

my past. The bull walks
knowing his way home.

I soak calluses, wash my feet
slow and methodical

between each toe, know
the journey is worth my salt.

Fault Line

And this is where I stop.
Where I begin again.

Repeated displacements
exposed roots underfoot,

trapped my worth in silence.
I move in relation, make

a fierce decision to believe
beyond what I feel.

Take the next step. Slow.
Stave off a sudden quake.

Reflective Narrator

And it seems
as I look back

having decided
to remember

what I did well,
earlier selves

guard the tomb
of suppressed memory.

With feet on fresh
ground, one heart

risking exposure
to the unknown,

there is no choice
only to forgive at all cost.

Smelling the Flowers

Loneliness is a lack of quality
in connection. I once made happiness
a plateau—nowhere to rise or fall.
Time progresses whether I solve
how to die without regret, or not.
When mercy plucks sinew and hears
cavernous echo, it's not enough to want
self-worth. It's to know what worth looks
like. So here I am, olfactory nerves
ready to give reprieve and stand exposed,
honey-cotton candy stirring absolution.

Many Worlds

I'm not arguing quantum mechanics.
But what about the split-second—

how days long years short is
an accumulation of parenting

over time. One minute I'm driving.
The next: jail. Or,

a local chef descends to the cellar,
busy preparing a celebratory feast,

trips. Dies. His arm reaching
for the refrigerator. I envision

he grabs cheese and deli meats
before skipping upstairs like I see

my friend passed out on the couch,
me in bed with a head-splitting hangover—

an infinite number of worlds
splintering—the crash,

not a choice but an elongated
series of occurrences set in motion

by choice. I drive by a woman
picking toys from dirt and dried

weeds in a chicken-wire fenced
yard on a desolate highway

and know the curve of her pelvis,
tangles in dingy hair, the knobby spine.

Too young for the weight carried
in grim eyes—both of us

spawned by a single split in time.

wrong /rôNG/

verb. Act unjustly or dishonestly toward: As in, it is clear I *wronged* his parents who burned the olive tree's branches; who pleaded for a strong and just punishment. It is clear I was *wronged* a chance to reconnect; an opportunity to transform tragedy into service; for rebirth. And isn't this the way—everyone thinking they know the right thing to do.

Gates of Ocala

Heading south the terrain is straight,
flat. Black post and rail fences divide

evergreen pastures and Thoroughbreds
cultivated in limestone-

rich soil. I know I'm close.
Off the highway, I enter

the suburban city, drive past
neighborhood after neighborhood

painted in neutral colors of Candler sand,
guided by the blue dot of GPS.

Before I turn off the main road.
Before the unknown's hand slaps me

with knowledge. I grow unsettled for the want
to knock on my father's front door.

The blinker clicks and ticks and counts
seconds until I steer

toward a neighborhood's mouth
that closes with the descent

of a barrier arm. I stop. Search
my emotional index for this scenario

I didn't plan for. A country club,
the guard in a square booth

with a clipboard, swarms of golf carts
racing after elusive white orbs,

the sun-kissed breeze
with undertones of moaning.

I travelled decades plus
six hundred miles to decide

this journey ends
without passing through the gate.

Just That Way

for MK

When a younger you asked
why no one says, *I love you,*

your mother acknowledged,
Some families are just that way.

A younger me heard my father
say those longed-for words

but he left and Mom said
he loved me in his own way,

teaching me words meant nothing,
really, and everything, also

because there you and I sat, laughing,
drinking beer with a sweaty June sunset,

ignorant to the night's tragic end, both of us
longing for the security we believed in love.

Dear Hindsight

Is that you again,
lurking in the hours
long and drawn?

Didn't we wrestle this one
the year I left
or the time when I should have
veered left but didn't?

It's just that
time blends together
like blue sky and brown trees
gray a canvas.

Maybe you need someone to talk to
like I need someone to listen.

I never know if this is it
between you and me

to move on is to expect
you in the mirror
judging every turn.

There Will Be Enough

Human reason is beautiful and invincible.
—Czesław Miłosz

To believe in a poem is to believe
in the mind at work like those
outside with a crane lifting
dredge pipes, keeping the beach
between house and sea.
With hard hat and caution
tape, lines siphon words
one end to the other
making reason I wouldn't have
otherwise, the ocean is too strong,
the house will wash away. Where else
can I find forgiveness
but in the repetition of pen
on paper, lifting what to consider
like stars lifted ancestral minds
out of peril to think
there is more than flesh and starlight.
It's hard to know when enough
is enough, whether it's time to enjoy
the sea at your doorstep, or dig.

Dear Universe

Whether I dig feet
into red clay dirt to grow

roots, cut detritus to clean
a hoarded mind, or memorize

the emergence of polychromatic
leaves and metallic layers of bark

as night lifts its veil,
there is nowhere to hide.

I follow sound to shape meaning,
push a grain of sand uphill and form nothing.

Choice can't steer my expectation train.
It doesn't have arms. Or control.

I dress to flatter. We dance or spar,
but you always have the first move.

Restoration

I must be shedding. Youth
insisted the journey was one long reach

toward an unknown character
who whisks you away—a hero

on horseback; the ocean tide.
There's so much more.

Like an annual ring secures a tree
deeper into place, my center of gravity lowers,

prepares for another year's growth.
Skin regenerates slower, but pliable.

Letting Go

I needed to return. This time
to watch red lights

brighten leaves and apartment
buildings in a halo marking

the spot—the car, the pole, the helpers
helping. To turn toward his body

knowing he won't walk away
from the car but he will build

a life upon those who carried him.
I needed to see our story

keep writing itself as I gathered
shards of my character,

found words that helped
me stop. Wait. And breathe.

Long enough to accept
I can walk away too.

Becoming Worthwhile

This burst like the iris
through mulch; this yearn
a long-tended fire burning
through generations; this
non-fallow season; this non-
harvest; this is not summer
heat when water is scarce;
this is renewal and not renewal;
this is the curve passed gestation
before budding; this is years'
work of forming into a life;
this is not the first time
this has happened; this is
the only time this happens.

Section II

Forgiveness is not an occasional act,
it is a permanent attitude.

—Martin Luther King, Jr.

Things

Weeds in the garden.
Clothesline, pine trees, azaleas,
honeysuckle along chain-link fence

toward camellia, pittosporum,
a shed. My grandmother's silver
tableware in a velvet box forgotten

on a dust-laden workbench,
never having a table proper
enough. Snakeskin,

concert tickets, letters,
a serpent lapel pin
I promised another to keep

safe from darkness, marbles
found at the tender age
of twenty—all meaning wiped

clean having almost killed
a friend by accident, the world
inside me larger than I imagined.

I don't know how I held on
to anything, really, but I wrapped
my hand around the once lost

blue and green swirled glass,
bought them a carved wood box
in triumph that wasn't yet mine.

Allowance

To forgive myself is to strip
shame's tendrils adhered to my bones
and muscle, its loud voice over the PA
system on repeat, *You are a bad thing*.
It's slow, methodical work
to reveal myself to myself
so I can walk into a moment where
I am ready to allow someone to love me.

Blind Date

There's no label
for the way

we reveal ourselves
on my balcony,

our desire to become
the person who stays

passing between us
like a field of fireflies.

Stuff

We don't know in our promise
written at the kitchen table

with our friend who will preside
over the wedding thanks to ordination

by internet, *stuff* isn't what we own.
I take your hand in mine. That is all.

Wellspring

Contentment—
possesses nothing,
regenerates cells.

1709 Center Road

From the beginning
we are pushed. Timestamped.

The sea turtle leaves the beach
connected by a magnetic force

to home as reservoir. An imprint.
1100 square feet plus a screened-in

front porch orients our blended
family to our own coordinates.

Mother and son. Husband.
Two dogs and one old cat.

Two babies arrive
twenty minutes apart, and time

stands still, as it tends to do—
both familiar and new, as I'm older now

watching my first born enter
the world inside himself.

The babies, born beyond a lifetime
they didn't experience, receive

our presence, instill their homing instinct.
This house, where we all begin again.

Grace in the Hills and Gardens

I was working toward forgiveness when,
next to a carton of eggs, expired yogurt
dismantled my self-worth, again.
When I said I was searching for Grace
I meant I wanted certainty for myself.
I'm glaring at the refrigerator,
arms crossed tight over my chest
when my husband walks in.
I've tried to be better, I say.
He guides my hands onto his ribs
where my thumbs move across resilience.
Let your guard down, he says,
stepping so our thighs touch. And I weep.
Crying I did alone in the shower
during my first marriage, or secluded at night
as a young single mother. Tears that roll
from the hills and gardens of a driver's seat,
where I once sat—suddenly sober—
next to a boisterous friend gone limp on impact.

Not Born Alone

Mom and I leave Vegas
sheltered by sky and herding fences.

Crosses cast shadows on towns of wood
and dust, on people long scattered

from isolation scratching at the door.
I'm moving her, this woman

who raised me to survive alone,
across the country to live

down the street as she declines.
Vultures tail us

through the Texas panhandle. A diner
advertises *homemade food*,

serves canned tomato soup.
Somewhere—I believe

margaritas in Albuquerque—
a zygote divides. Windmills

dot the horizon spinning.
A man walks the interstate,

child's wagon tied to a strap
across his torso, sun hat snug

over ears, eyes up and forward,
beard grazing a firm, lean chest.

And I know
I am more he, a lone

tattered wanderer, then a constant
companion like the two

growing in mirror relation
in my womb. I don't know the rules

for babies born into connection so strong
it's a third entity I will swaddle. I will feed.

I will lie awake at night while they sleep,
tending to its illusion.

Synchronous

I coax sleep to beget
sleep, train

two-month-olds
to remember one

circadian rhythm,
condition myself

to remain steady.
My rhythmic hands

one on each infant
in chairs that give

a little bounce.
The three of us

birthed into a world
where we cannot see

but twelve inches
past our noses.

(Re) Memory

A son's head rests
in the cradle
of my collarbone.

My arm wraps
around bony shoulder.
The weight of his leaning.

A movie's on, but

the weight of his leaning.
Around bony shoulder,
my arm wraps.

Of my collarbone,
in the cradle,
a son's head rests.

for · give /fərˈgiv/

verb. Stop feeling angry or resentful toward (someone) for an offense, flaw, or mistake: As in, I am in the process of surrender—hands up, I have laid down my weapon; hands on the ground in prostration; I yield to shame that is synonymous with my name; set aside an ego full of answers; bring forth, make room for, become a well of fresh water filling every bucket that comes to collect; as the sum of my actions, and in the presence of non-action, I walk hand-in-hand with the past that cannot be changed, turn to myself and say, "Let me be in the presence of you; let me be the source of acceptance that says, I *forgive* you."

Origins

I need to visit the one-lane
dead-end road on a small
cinder cone mountain wrapped
by a river moving beyond town
entering the ocean between
sunbathing seals to recall why
I define thinking as water.

Rapture I

Sonoma Coast, California

Toes assess sturdiness
for my full weight
on blue-gray boulders
abutting cliffside.
Warm sun, cold hands
climb, tucked
along the shore's
gush and *swoosh*,
where I can't hear
if my name is called,
a seclusion discovered
as a child on these rocks
where no one followed.
Just me and sleeper
waves, and how
leaving makes me
see everything
as I left it.

When I Leave the Protection of the Grocery Store Aisle

Stand exposed in the fresh foods section,
the savanna of the store, seen from checkout

aisles and a side entrance, the deli counter
and coffee bar. Shopping basket clamped

in the elbow, lone artichoke nested in a corner,
picked for the way it takes me to kneeling

at the coffee table as a child, dipping
leaves in melted butter. Decide on chowder

to eat with the second sourdough boule bought
during an unseasonably cold first of March,

a winter of river-storms salving scars
from drought and fire. And that is when I hear her

say my name in the employee-owned co-op
that didn't exist when I lived

in this agricultural wine country
where I don't know who I know anymore,

both at home and out of sorts
as I look into her face and feel

years deepen the lines on my own.
The one person I want to know my story.

Ecosystem

I sink into oak trees, shrinking bones.
A stream trickles down the mountainside,
birds, green moss, wood stairs descend
to the crackled road, musty-wet
but little algae. We're together,
childhood friends rewiring one another
into our adult lives, like a flower opens
for the insect it needs to survive.
Air is dust dry. Trees, thirty years taller.
The cemetery less haunted.
When I finally catch a smell it's pine,
sense the lush South that awaits my return,
move through the valley landscape that shaped
my early ways of believing in the world.
Redwood skyscrapers root to dark soil.
We made it this far, dear friend, to explore
what it means to have so much time left,
the unabashed joy in a face from long ago.
Pure presence. We're thirty years taller too.

Drought

The grass doesn't smell.
Neither do river rocks or the granite sand.

Water moves, a conveyor belt
of *hum* and *shush*, steady,

fat with rain. I'm looking to connect
but there's no parking here—

Silicon money bought houses
sinking down the mountain

where I slept pre-teen, water cradling
men standing riverside to please themselves.

At least we knew the boogeyman
walked pre-dawn, looking for his cat. At least

we allowed visitors.
I roam the mountainside to explain how

what I search for becomes what I miss—
decaying plant matter, life giving way

to new life, the whole body in conversation.
I know the view out these windows.

Watched bedroom furniture float by,
witnessed hope overcome flood.

Arrival

My body hears everything I think.
It's listening for cracked soil
that cannot drink fast enough.

A sixteen-year-old wants
more than food and shelter
from her mother, desire from men—

a way to be more than body.
When my memory doesn't comply,
the body adjusts like houses

swollen with humidity find equilibrium
in the air, eventually settle
into the dry season. I'm here

because I keep returning.
Unannounced,
I am in forgiveness.

It's not fancy, just a word that brings
my breath to a crushing stop.
Like hands of a lover ensures my presence,

estrogen gathers around my uterus,
protects it from the absence of life.
I returned home to find something I lost.

Found shame kept me away.
I perform salutations to an audience
of no one, bow to showing up.

Yellow

A butterfly carries another winter
river-storm to the Sonoma Coast,
flits like a late summer kite
over the marine terrace. Water
pounds outcrops into black sand,
reverberates full and deep and high-pitched—
Nature's opera leaves no room for words
I am here to find. And so.
Butterfly. Kite. My garden back east.
Mom's ashes planted with gladiolas,
her favorite color, yellow, bloomed first,
indicating she Is. Sticky notes. A monarch.
The highlighter I move across pages
to say, *This is important.*

The Nature of Lying Down

Before I kneel
in morning silence,

separate twins'
slumbered like magnets,

I dwell on commas
halting words like midnight

pauses the perpetuation
of days. Sometimes,

I linger in bed thinking
homemade blankets are entwined

with fingerprints and minutes,
stardust tucks in stardust,

and how will I ever lie down
without getting back up?

Omens

There are crows in every town.
I didn't know loving something so easily
was a sign to stick with it, fight to keep it,

that fitting worth in a pocket
makes it certain I can carry its weight.
I welcome the bees who know

what's good for them—trumpet flowers
play their song in June, feed the world
even if no one listens. When it's summer

in my body, remove socks and sweater.
When the weather cools, put them back on.
Repeat, all day, as necessary.

The Ceasing

We wait in the rush of the crisp stream,
enveloped in white noise, the children

up to their waists. Over stone and steady flow,
we make exhilaration.

No one says a word. The water speaks clearly.
At a window, looking out, I'm at odds

with the sitting that allows me to write.
My appetite is in reverse, my softened belly

folds skin into itself. I set the table over and again
to keep gathering. The oven is hot. The children

are called to a future they will look after.
It took moons to make a home for them to return to.

It takes years sometimes, to learn the shoe
has its own gravitational pull, its own

downward descent. Loss is everywhere
in the house: the lifespan of animals, one sock

from three different pairs, memories.
Release, too: a lightened mind, an explosive *yes*,

the curiosity it takes to find.
I handle this body at the mercy of paper

slicing flesh. Scavengers wait for my decay.
I forget how enticing the smell of blood.

Phone Notes

I choose to forgive the man
who licked my back.

Another, with fumbling
fingers in my underwear

while I slept, hoped for
legs spread like the eagle

who dominates countries. When
we're not at war we're at war

with ourselves. It's never futile
to walk as a woman. And yet,

I can't fathom childhood
where math equations and verbs

barricade doors. Walking my kids
to school—the two from one egg

who don't know existential
loneliness—I don't have words to explain

someone might shoot them for an idea.
For immortalization.

We're taught to slather
perfection on wrinkles,

hoard resources and opportunity
on piles of land saying, *Mine.*

A lecher's search for meaning
turns to control over another,

served to him at breakfast
when he's ordered not to cry.

Salt of the Earth

We arrive in Chloride, AZ,
my first born and I on our own

vacation. He, an adult.
I, more than Mother.

Salt of the earth, the caretaker says,
nodding toward the local drunk

outside room six on the Inn's
hundred-year-old porch,

his head sunk low, shoulders
the humped shape of vulture

wings cocked, his worth
connected to ancestors who followed

animals to the white veins of Earth,
who fished in dried-up seas.

Every generation is paid in scarcity,
licks wounds with salt.

We'll all sleep here tonight,
between adobe walls twelve inches thick

nothing can get you but
the journey that led you here.

I've Got You

My eldest says. His brothers,
a generation younger, want
to explore YouTube's expanse
with all those portals sending
them to worlds I don't know
well enough. I'm too saturated
by a petal's tenderness, the flower's
ecosystem. I fear the internet may
cause my brain to explode.
I keep talking and he keeps saying,
I've got you, words I've said
every time he went to leap or between
the lines of an ordinary day.
I've got you, like a baton between us,
this man at the helm of generations
I will never see, assimilates
the phrase and for a moment
I'm taking my last taste of breath
and he's there, as I was, with my own
mother lying on her deathbed, saying,
It's okay, you've done your work here.

Dear North Carolina

I'm sorry it took me so long to write.
I confess I never meant to stay.

You took off my shoes, walked me
barefoot on soft shoreline,
showed me how to vacation
on any given Tuesday,
the ease of a shovel
in shifting ground. Ah!
All the moon rises we've seen.

I've moved inland, as you know.

Red clay marks its territory
on everything it touches.
It's unforgiving but holds
tubers tight. My bearded irises
never looked better. I've never
looked better. Your vigorous
landscape relentless in giving
to maturity. After all these years,
your dust and sand are my bones.

I'm not of your land but I give
back to you with my own.

And I Don't Have to Think Anymore

after Jack Kerouac

It's the kind of rain that breaks morning fog,
tells me love is a floating seed
with so much at stake. I admit to driving

through Florida's sprawl of horse farms
and gated communities. It's like picking
from a flock of pigeons, all the retired

men in golf carts whizzing down
city streets, forgetting how to stand up
straight. All of them different versions

of my father peeling off white gloves,
and me, behind a rack of women's
fluorescent polos, summoning his name.

Every generation assimilates to their history.
I can't draw a straight line with a ruler
but I fold underwear in perfect squares.

It's the *good glad* rain, blooming,
releasing every decision into memory,
and I don't have to think anymore.

Rapture II

North Carolina seashore

Rush, swoop, crash, shush, shhhhhh. . .
Voices with wind, the clock melts.
Sea oats wave, the dunes hold.
Under pelican wings, light swirls,
water opens and closes
its mouth on the lollipop of land.
The ocean draws its own lines.
Sea froth melts back
into the great mother,
salty in how she carves
and collects me. How she
tumbles shells under the island
where dark means ancient,
wise, and *who you are*
matters more. I sink
into warm fine sand,
maritime forest and chair
on a screened-in porch,
present, and accounted for.

Heartwood

Our marriage settles
into middle-age.

Our bodies show us
deterioration isn't for others.

This home that we are
to one another, holds

together, strong as steel,
growing from the inside out.

I am Here. You are Here.

The inner thigh
slight cool of the stomach

fingers skip
the length of you

type back up
palms down, my hands

pulse like one heart
invoking

lover, healer
looking over your quiver of lines

your bare expression
of surprise

the two of us, saving ourselves
with witness.

Ocean Affirmation

I wake early
to say good morning,
sometimes with a slight nod,

edges of my mouth
turned up, or a half wave,
hand no higher

than my chest.
Greetings that sway
with ole salty blue,

balmy and reliable,
the shoreline shifting
beneath a steady pace.

Yes, it is good.
Yes, it is morning.
Yes.

References

Epigraphs and the use of a word or phrase in a poem are included here. Words and phrases used inside a poem are italicized. In the case where a word or phrase is used as a title, there are no italics. Some references are for informational purposes only. References in order of appearance.

Robbins, Tom. *Still Life with Woodpecker*. Bantam Books, 1981.

SECTION I

Bach, Richard. *One*. Dell Publishing, 1988.

"Learning to Forgive"
Chaddha, Rima and Audrey Resutek. "Secrets of the samurai sword: making a masterpiece." PBS NOVA. Published August 2007. https://pbs.org/wgbh/nova/samurai/swor-nf.html

"For Years I Pulled My Existence Out of Emptiness"
Rumi. "The World Which Is Made of Our Love for Emptiness." In *Rumi Poems*. Edited by Peter Washington. Alfred A. Knopf, 2006.

"I Am What I Can"
Descartes, René. *Selections from the Principles of Philosophy*, part 1, article VII. Translated by John Veitch. Produced by Steve Harris, Charles Franke, and the Online Distributed Proofreading Team at Project Gutenberg. Last modified June 17, 2024. https://gutenberg.org/ebooks/4391. EPUB.

"To Be of Use"
Nietzsche, Friedrich. *The Gay Science*, book 4. New edition. E.W. Fritzsch, 1887. Accessed November 5, 2020. https://web.stanford.edu/~jsabol/existentialism/materials/nietzsche-gay-science-hurry.pdf [Author's note: The quote I used is edited into active voice without losing context of meaning from the original.]

"Wilder Family Crest"
Wilder, Moses Hale. *Book of the Wilders*. Revised edition. Compiled by
Edwin M. Wilder, MD. 1975-76. In the author's possession. [Author's
note: A genealogical history from 1497, in England, to the immigration
of Martha, a widow and her family, to Massachusetts Bay, in 1638,
and so through her family down to 1875. The first edition was printed
in 1878. The revised edition continues the genealogical history to the
early 1970s. The copy I have was typed on a typewriter and put in
three-ring binders.]

"Complaint of Shelter"
Blanco, Richard. "Complaint of El Rio Grande." In *How to Love a
Country*. Beacon Press, 2019.

"Fault Line"
"What is a fault and what are the different types." U.S. Geological
Survey, U.S. Department of the Interior. Last modified April 8, 2025.
https://www.usgs.gov/faqs/what-a-fault-and-what-are-different-types

"Gates of Ocala"
Alighieri, Dante. *The Divine Comedy of Dante Alighieri: Inferno*.
Translated by Allen Mandelbaum. Bantam Books, 1982.

"There Will Be Enough"
Miłosz, Czesław. "Incantation." In *The Collected Poems 1931-1987*.
Translated by Czesław Miłosz and Robert Pinsky. The Ecco Press,
1988.

SECTION II

King, Martin Luther, Jr. Draft of Chapter IV, "Love in Action."
Atlanta, Georgia. 1962-63. The Martin Luther King, Jr. Research
and Education Center at Stanford University. Accessed October 10,
2024. https://kinginstitute.stanford.edu/king-papers/documents/
draft-chapter-iv-love-action

"Grace in the Hills and Gardens"
Anthony, Carol K. "Pi, Grace (Hexagram 22)." In *A Guide to the I Ching*. Third edition. Anthony Publishing Company, 1988.

"And I Don't Have to Think Anymore"
Kerouac, Jack. "How to Meditate." In *The Portable Jack Kerouac*. Edited by Ann Charters. Penguin Publishing Group, 2007.

Acknowledgments

I want to thank the readers of *Anything That Happens* who asked me, "Have you forgiven yourself?" Your questions inspired me to explore how I came to self-forgiveness. This collection is an examination of the process, and it wouldn't exist without your curiosity and support.

I'm grateful to have received an artist support grant from the North Carolina Arts Council, a division of the Department of Natural and Cultural Resources, with funding from the National Endowment for the Arts and Durham Arts Council, local grants administrator. The grant made it possible to travel to my hometown in California, providing the opportunity to reconnect with the terrain through writing and explore old stomping grounds with Eric Nichols, a childhood friend and photographer. Many thanks to the North Carolina Poetry Society for accepting "Ocean Affirmation" to appear in its Poetry in Plain Sight, to Alamance Arts for including "Letter to Alamance County" (now in a slightly different form and renamed "Letter to North Carolina") in their *Eyes on Alamance* exhibit, to the Alamance County Public Libraries for accepting "Rapture II," "Wellspring," "Origins," and "Reflective Narrator" to appear in the Alamance County Poetry Stroll, and to Old Mountain Press for including "Season 2022" (now in a slightly different form and renamed "Becoming Worthwhile") in their *Joy to All* anthology and "Drought" in their *Mountain Lakes* anthology.

Community has been crucial to my growing sense of belonging and connection.

Heartfelt thanks to readers who helped shape individual poems, including members of the Burlington Writers Club poetry critique group. Huge thanks to Steve Cushman who read the full manuscript and offered crucial developmental advice and to Barbara Presnell, Rita Lewis, Nicole Gulotta, and Debra Kaufman who helped with final revisions.

Acknowledgments

Support comes in many forms.

To Karin Wiberg, Jenni Hart, and Rita Lewis for their friendship and business acumen, which helped me grow into an entrepreneur on my own terms. To my sinners-in-writing, Claire Guyton and Suzanne Farrell Smith, who, for thirteen years, have walked with me during the tough moments and soothed my spirit so I could keep going. And to Coleen Tagnolli, for asking me if I wanted to be her friend when I was the new kid in sixth grade: Thank you for always being game for a dance party and gracing this book with your stunning artwork. Special appreciation goes to Molly's Place, an oceanside refuge where I write and recuperate, thanks to the ever-gracious Bill Shipman and the Shipman family.

To my publicist, Hannah Larrew, who blends enthusiasm and hard work seamlessly. And my editor and publisher, Kevin Watson, who is a champion for his Press 53 authors, a steward of the written word, and an overall kind person and friend. Thank you both for believing in my work.

To all my friends and family: Your encouragement, honesty, laughter, and patience is deeply appreciated. You make me rich beyond measure.

Lastly, and always, to Taliesin, Evander, and Roland, who show me through their imaginations, empathy, and deep sensitivity what it means to feel fully and completely alive. And Danny, who grounds me, uplifts me, and cooks dinner. Our home makes it all possible.

About the Author

Singing Riptide charts Cheryl Wilder's journey from personal, all-consuming shame; through the intergenerational forgiveness that made self-forgiveness possible; to self-realization and belonging. A companion to *Anything That Happens* (Press 53)—the collection that chronicles the root of Wilder's shame and how she navigated the immediate aftermath—*Singing Riptide* was supported by the North Carolina Arts Council, a division of the Department of Natural and Cultural Resources, with funding from the National Endowment for the Arts and Durham Arts Council, local grants administrator. *Anything That Happens*, a Tom Lombardo Poetry Selection, was named Second Finalist in the Poetry Society of Virginia North American Book Award and received Honorable Mention in the Brockman-Campbell Book Award. Cheryl is the author of the chapbook, *What Binds Us* (Finishing Line Press), and her work appears in Poetry in Plain Sight, Alamance Arts *Eyes on Alamance* community exhibit, *Crossing the Rift: North Carolina Poets on 9/11 & Its Aftermath* (Press 53), *Joy to All* and *Mountain Lakes* anthologies (Old Mountain Press), *Barely South Review, Cream City Review*, and *Architects + Artisans*, among others. Cheryl is a North Carolina Poetry Society board member, a community guide in the For Alamance Initiative, past president of the Burlington Writers Club and co-chair of their Student Writing Contest. A recipient of a Sundress Academy for the Arts residency, Cheryl has served as writer-in-residence for *SistaWRITE*. Her education includes a BFA from UNC Wilmington and MFA from Vermont College of Fine Arts. The owner of BornWilder LLC, Cheryl coach's clients to envision aspirations by tapping into their authenticity and shares her experiences with shame and forgiveness as a speaker, inspiring others to embrace their unique passions and purpose. Find her at bornwilder.com

About the Cover Artist

Cover artist Coleen Tagnolli is a wife, mother, nurse by profession, and artist at heart. At thirty-seven years old, Coleen was diagnosed with a rare breast cancer, and her odds of survival were slim. In the aftermath of her battle, playing with paint was a healing force that helped her embrace life on its terms while also allowing her to redefine and embrace a post-cancer version of herself. Born and raised in Northern California, Coleen lives and paints in North Carolina.

www.ingramcontent.com/pod-product-compliance
Lightning Source LLC
Chambersburg PA
CBHW021509090426
42739CB00007B/539